Primary Inquirer series
Teacher's Resources

Senses

Lesley and Kenneth Snowball

Pearson in partnership with Putting it into Practice

Pearson Education Limited is a company incorporated in England and Wales, having its registered office at Edinburgh Gate, Harlow, Essex, CM20 2JE. Registered company number: 872828

www.pearsonschoolsandfecolleges.co.uk

Developed from an original concept by Putting it into Practice
Text © Putting it into Practice
Artwork and Design © Pearson Education Ltd, 2010

British Library Cataloguing in Publication Data
A catalogue record for this book is available from the British Library

First published 2010

13 12 11 10
10 9 8 7 6 5 4 3 2 1

ISBN 9780435018238

Copyright notice
All rights reserved. The material in this publication is copyright. Student sheets may be freely photocopied for classroom use in the purchasing institution. However, this material is copyright and under no circumstances may copies be offered for sale. If you wish to use the material in any way other than that specified you must apply in writing to the publishers.

Designed and typeset by K and S Design © Pearson Education Ltd, 2010
Illustrated by Shelagh McNicholas © Pearson Education Ltd, 2010
Cover design by Creative Monkey © Pearson Education Ltd, 2010
Picture research by Kevin Brown
Printed in the UK

Acknowledgements
The publisher would like to thank the following for their kind permission to reproduce their photographs:
Photodisc: Photolink Contents page

Every effort has been made to trace the copyright holders and we apologise in advance for any unintentional omissions. We would be pleased to insert the appropriate acknowledgement in any subsequent edition of this publication.

An inquiry into: Senses

Contents

General introduction 2

How can we plan for inquiry (Planning organisers) 3

Defining the unit 4

The strand grid 5

The integration web 6

The multiple intelligences grid 7

The organising theme model 8

The concept questions taxonomy 9

The learning centres framework 10

The unit of inquiry planner 11

Supplementary materials 13

Blank unit of inquiry planner 13

Putting it into practice with parents 15

Student resource sample sheets 16

Early Years sample sheets 16

Lower Primary sample sheets 18

Upper Primary sample sheets 20

An inquiry into: Senses

General introduction

The Primary Inquirer series

Pearson Putting it into Practice Primary Inquirer series units are time-saving springboards helping busy teachers plan thematic inquiry-based units. They provide an ideal basis for collaborative planning across and between year levels and subject areas. Titles in the **Primary Inquiry** series include:

An inquiry into:

Art	Fitness	Food	Games	Legacies
Mapping	Materials	Money	Music	My country
Numbers	Pattern	Plants	Poetry	Senses
Stories	Time	Transport	Water	Weather

For every unit, there is a Teacher resources book and a choice of Student resources.

Teacher resources

The teacher resources include a variety of different planning organisers, designed to complement different curriculum models (for example, PYP, IPC, England National Curriculum). These offer a full support base for teachers new to inquiry and supplementary time-saving ideas for experienced teachers. Teacher resource sheets are labelled with the Primary Inquirer hexagon which indicates the organising themes receiving the primary focus in this unit. The resources can be used both as discrete units and to supplement other units, and the series builds into a full programme of inquiry, providing a valuable set of resources.

Student resources

The student resource CD-ROMs are designed specifically for an inquiry-based classroom. The resources are organised into three age bands:

- Early Years
- Lower Primary
- Upper Primary

Each student resources CD-ROM contains:

- **Starter activities** to help students tune-in to the unit: activating prior knowledge, making connections and stimulating vocabulary.
- **Main activities** to provide frameworks and formats to guide students through structured inquiry: within each age band the main activities are differentiated to provide 3 levels of support and challenge for diverse student needs.
- **Summarising activities** to round off the unit in a purposeful manner: synthesising learning, encouraging reflection and providing closure.
- **Assessment sheets** to monitor and record student learning: using a range of formative, summative and self-assessment tasks before, during and after the unit.
- **Homework activities** to consolidate and extend in-school learning: involving parents with research, skills practice and language development.

The CD-ROMs are available separately or can be used together for more extensive coverage.

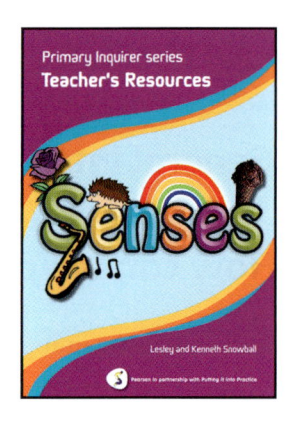

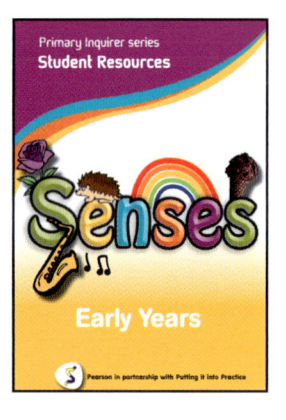

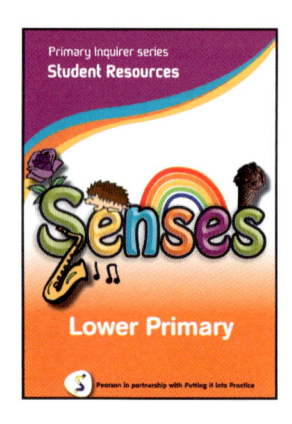

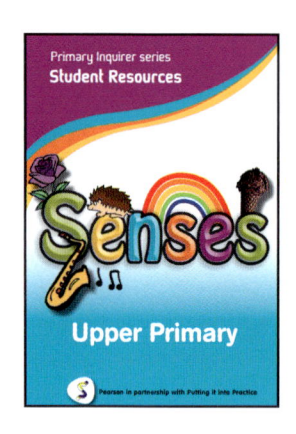

An inquiry into: Senses

How can we plan for inquiry?

Planning organisers

Depending on how your school organises curriculum and plans units of study, an inquiry can be approached from several different angles, as shown by the following planning organisers:

- **Defining the unit** considers what the unit is, why it is worth inquiring into, what aspects are most important and what methods might be used
- **The strand grid** shows mathematics and language strands that could be integrated at different age levels: the language ideas are particularly useful for working with ESL students, as they indicate possible areas of specific language and literature focus within the unit
- **The integration web** shows potential transdisciplinary connections, and is particularly useful for specialist teachers aiming to integrate their specific subject objectives into an integrated topic
- **The multiple intelligences grid** suggests questions to help teachers differentiate by engaging students' diverse intelligence profiles
  The titles of the seven intelligences are based on the original theory of multiple intelligences by Howard Gardner.
- **The organising theme model** shows the key inquiry points that could be investigated in each of six organising themes. PYP schools need to choose one theme on which the unit will focus. Boyer's original concept, on which the PYP themes are based, considered that addressing each theme would represent a balance of all areas of knowledge, but did not determine a specific number of units to be taught each year. Therefore, used flexibly, the themes can facilitate transdisciplinary integration and are a very useful organising tool for any inquiry-based school
  The titles of the six organising themes are taken from the International Schools Curriculum Project publication *Making it happen in the classroom* which was based on *The Educated Person* by Ernst Boyer.
- **The concept questions taxonomy** is arranged according to the eight key concepts used in the PYP framework. The questions and these eight concepts are hierarchical, and provide a very useful tool for any inquiry-based classroom. It is important to ensure that over a series of units, questions are included from across the eight concepts; especially the higher level, more abstract concepts of perspective, responsibility and reflection
  The titles of the eight concepts are based on the International Schools Curriculum Project publication *Making it happen in the classroom*.
- **The learning centres framework** provides an effective way to structure inquiry, allowing students to work in groups, pairs or individually to investigate different aspects of the unit. Depending on the space and time available, the learning centres shown here can be organised to address different lines of inquiry simultaneously, or to focus on one aspect at a time with activities differentiated for a range of abilities
- **The unit of inquiry planner** provides an outline for teaching the unit of inquiry, identifying concepts, skills, knowledge and attitudes to be addressed, as well as key questions, activities, assessments and resources. For PYP schools, it focuses on the organising theme(s) indicated.

© Putting it into Practice. Artwork and Design © Pearson Education Ltd, 2010

An inquiry into: Senses

Defining the unit

> **Defining the unit** considers what the unit is, why it is worth inquiring into, what aspects are most important and what methods might be used.

What is it?
Our five senses of **sight**, **hearing**, **smell**, **taste** and **touch** are our means of gathering (and expressing) information about the world.

Why inquire into it?
Because our senses are so fundamental to our lives, it is important that we understand how they work, what they can do, and how we can take care of them. It is a good topic for any classroom, needing only simple, easily-available resources. It is accessible to all children and lends itself to open-ended, student-initiated investigation.

What aspects should we inquire into?
- time
- vision
- hearing
- smell
- touch
- taste
- magic
- tricking
- optical
- illusion
- perception
- memories
- the brain
- memory

An inquiry into: Senses

The strand grid

> **The strand grid** shows mathematics and language strands that could be integrated at different age levels: the language ideas are particularly useful for working with ESL students, as they indicate possible areas of specific language and literature focus within the unit.

		Age 3 →		→ Age 12
Mathematics	Data handling	• collect and organise concrete data • record data using real objects, pictures and symbols	• collect and generate data • record data using a range of simple recording methods • interpret data	• collecting and generating data / record data selecting appropriate methods according to purpose • interpretations (plausible, possible, impossible) • predictions • extrapolations
	Measurement	• develop simple scales to measure taste etc. • use senses to gather data	• estimation and measurement in experiments	• use of measurement tools and equipment
	Number	• basic vocabulary same/different, big/little • comparative vocabulary more/less, bigger, longer, higher	• estimation • qualifying vocabulary almost, nearly, exactly, mostly	• use four operations
	Pattern and function	• recognition, creation and extension of single attribute patterns	• recognition, creation and extension of multiple attribute patterns	• recognition, creation and extension of complex patterns
	Reasoning	• solve simple logic problems • simple if-then statements • sorting, comparing and ordering according to simple criteria	• solve and create simple logic problems • if-then statements • sorting, comparing and ordering with multiple criteria	• logic problems • sort, compare, order with complex criteria
Language	Shape and space	• recognising and naming shapes • 2-D and 3-D shapes • simple tessellations • simple reflective symmetry	• identifying the attributes of 2-D and 3-D shapes • tessellations • symmetry	• complex tessellations • complex symmetry
	Metalanguage	• Vocabulary simple nouns and adjectives • present tense – what's happening?	• Vocabulary adjectives and adverbs • past tense – what happened and why?	• more complex vocabulary • future and conditional tenses – what will/could happen if?
	Literature	• picture information books • fairy tales	• poems • information books / fiction	• genre fiction • biographies
	Language across the curriculum	• names of senses • associated descriptive words	• science process vocabulary	• scientific names for body parts and processes

© Putting it into Practice. Artwork and Design © Pearson Education Ltd, 2010

An inquiry into: Senses

The integration web

The integration web shows potential transdisciplinary connections, and is particularly useful for specialist teachers aiming to integrate their specific subject objectives into an integrated topic.

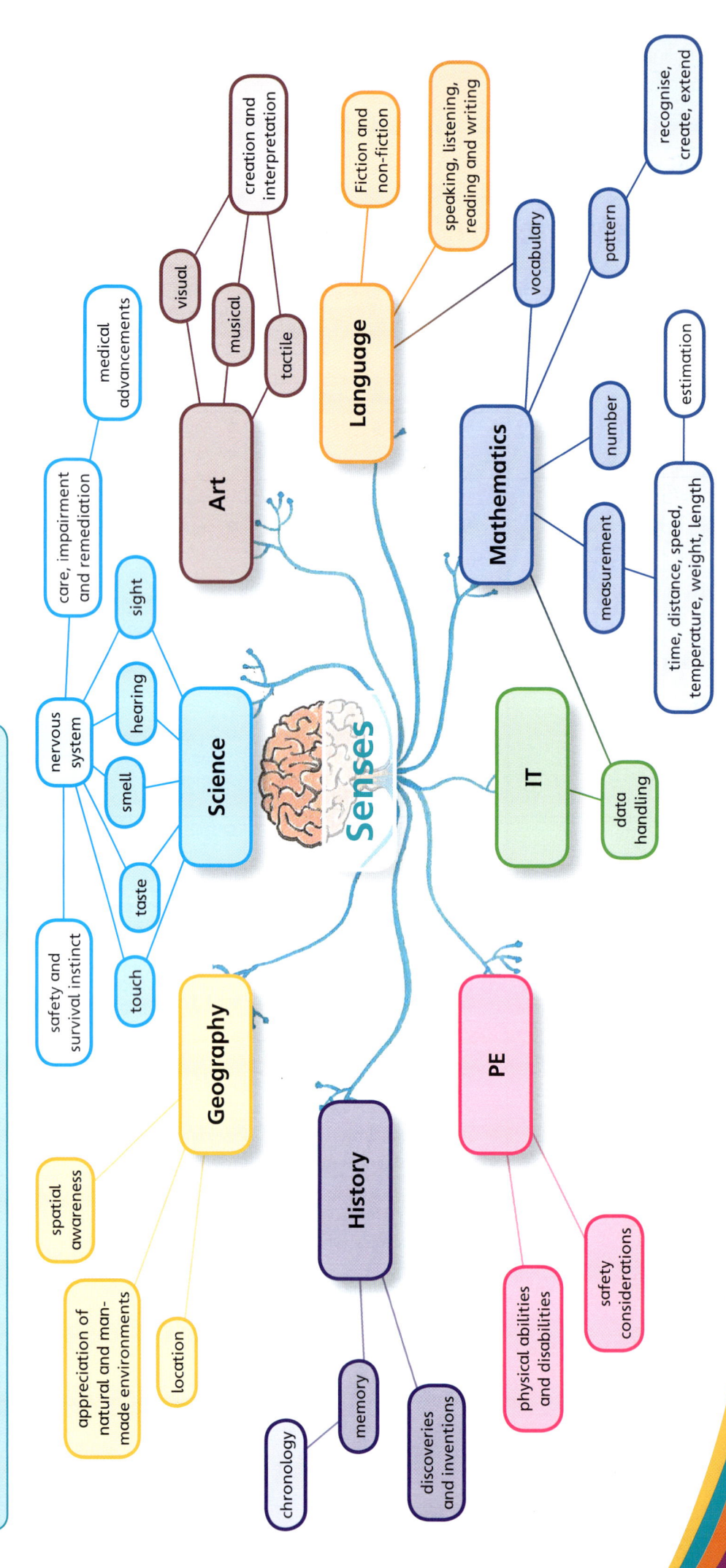

Senses

- **Art**
  - creation and interpretation
    - visual
    - musical
    - tactile
  - medical advancements

- **Language**
  - Fiction and non-fiction
  - speaking, listening, reading and writing
  - vocabulary

- **Mathematics**
  - pattern
    - recognise, create, extend
  - number
    - estimation
  - measurement
    - time, distance, speed, temperature, weight, length

- **Science**
  - care, impairment and remediation
  - nervous system
    - sight
    - hearing
    - smell
    - taste
    - touch
  - safety and survival instinct

- **IT**
  - data handling

- **Geography**
  - spatial awareness
  - appreciation of natural and man-made environments
  - location

- **History**
  - chronology
  - memory
  - discoveries and inventions

- **PE**
  - physical abilities and disabilities
  - safety considerations

An inquiry into: Senses

The multiple intelligences grid

The multiple intelligences grid suggests questions to help teachers differentiate by engaging students' diverse intelligence profiles.

Linguistic	• What are your senses called? • What parts of the body are used? • How do we learn to speak? • How many different languages are there? • Which can you speak? • How do we hear someone else speaking? • What kinds of words describe what we see? Hear? Feel? Taste? Smell? • What senses do we use to listen, speak, read and write?
Logical – Mathematical	• How many senses do we have? • What body parts / systems do they use? • How many taste buds do we have? • How many nerve endings? • How do our senses help us to do mathematics? • How far can we see? Hear? • What animals have the best sight? Hearing? Touch? Smell? Taste?
Spatial	• How do our senses affect our spatial awareness? • Which senses tell us where we are? • How do our senses detect / control our movement, speed, direction? • How do open / closed spaces affect our senses?
Bodily – Kinesthetic	• How do our senses work? • How are they connected to the rest of our body? • Why are they important? • What kinds of problems can we have with our senses? • What happens if we lose the use of one of them? • How do our senses change as we grow older?
Musical	• How do our senses help us to appreciate music? • How can deaf people 'hear'? • Why are some people more musical than others? • What kinds of music do you like to listen to? • What kinds do you not like? • How do our musical preferences change as we develop?
Interpersonal	• How do our senses help us connect with other people? • Which do we use most? • Which other people help us take care of our senses? • Which jobs would be most suitable for people with good sight? Hearing? Touch? Taste? Smell?
Intrapersonal	• Which is your strongest sense? • Which do you think is most important? • How can you develop your senses? • How do you need to take care of your senses?

© Putting it into Practice. Artwork and Design © Pearson Education Ltd, 2010

An inquiry into: Senses

The organising theme model

The organising theme model shows the key inquiry points that could be investigated in each of six organising themes. PYP schools need to choose one theme on which the unit will focus. Boyer's original concept, on which the PYP themes are based, considered that addressing each theme would represent a balance of all areas of knowledge, but did not determine a specific number of units to be taught each year. Therefore, used flexibly, the themes can facilitate transdisciplinary integration and are a very useful organising tool for any inquiry-based school.

Who we are
- The five senses – sight, hearing, taste, touch, smell
- Taking care of our senses
- Perception
- Individual strengths and weaknesses
- Learning styles

Where we are in place and time
- Senses change as we grow
- A sense of time and place
- Contextual effects on the senses e.g. culture, location, darkness, fear
- Senses connected with our memory

How we express ourselves
- Using our senses to receive and express information
- Audio-visual media – art, sculpture, TV and radio, drama, dance, mime, puppetry
- Fooling the senses – magic and illusion

How the world works
- How sight (hearing, smell, taste, touch) works
- What happens when they don't work?
- Impact of technology
- Other creatures' senses
- Camouflage
- Perception and misperception

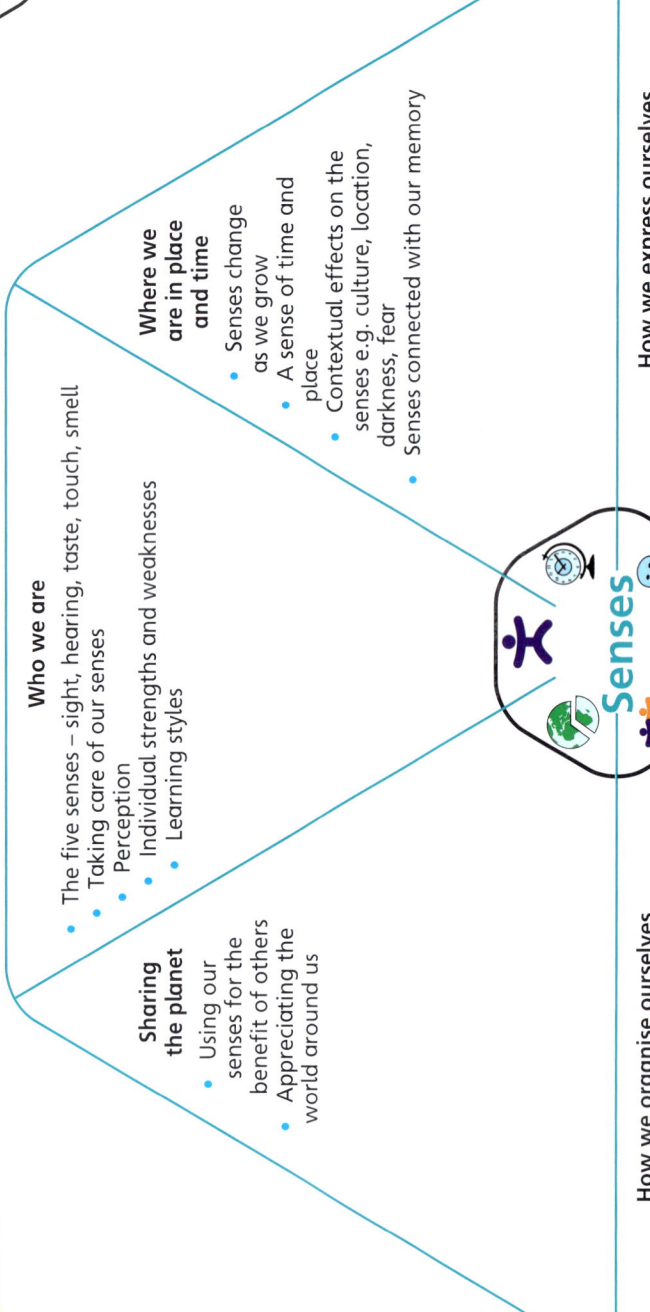

How we organise ourselves
- How do we manage when our senses don't work?
- Rights and responsibilities – safety, health care, respect
- Jobs connected to the senses – medical, dental, artists, chilli pepper taster, musician (perfect pitch)

Sharing the planet
- Using our senses for the benefit of others
- Appreciating the world around us

Senses

An Inquiry into: Senses

The concept questions taxonomy

The concept questions taxonomy is arranged according to the eight key concepts used in the PYP framework. The questions and these eight concepts are hierarchical, and provide a very useful tool for any inquiry-based classroom. It is important to ensure that over a series of units, questions are included from across the eight concepts; especially the higher level, more abstract concepts of perspective, responsibility and reflection.

Form	Function	Causation	Change	Connection	Perspective	Responsibility	Reflection
What is it like?	*How does it work?*	*Why is it the way it is?*	*How does it change?*	*How is it connected to other things?*	*What are the points of view? What are the ways of looking at it?*	*What is our responsibility?*	*How do we know?*
• What are senses? • What is sight? Hearing? Touch? Taste? Smell? • What does this look (sound, feel, taste, smell) like? • Which animals have the best sense of sight? Hearing? Taste? Smell? Touch?	• How does sight (hearing, touch, taste, smell) work? • What happens if one of our senses does not work? • How does our sense of time work?	• Why do we have these senses? • Why do we lose some senses as we get older? • Why do some animals have better senses than we do?	• How do our senses change in different contexts? • How does our sight change with distance? Time of day? Age? • How might human senses change in the future?	• How do the senses send information to the brain? • How can the senses work together? • How can the senses compensate for each other? • How do we remember smells, textures etc? • How are technological developments used to enhance or compensate for our senses?	• Which sense is most important to you? • Is this the same for everyone? • Which are your strongest senses? • Does everyone see (hear, feel, taste, smell) the same things? • What is an illusion? • What are your favourite sights? Sounds? Smells? Tastes? Textures?	• How can we take care of our senses? • What affects how well our senses work? • What can people do if one of their senses doesn't work? • Who is responsible for helping people whose senses don't work? • How can we help people who are sensorially deprived? • Is it acceptable to test products on animals if it benefits humans?	• How can we know what it's like to have senses that don't work? • How can we learn about our senses? • Do plants have senses? • How important is medical research for learning about the senses? • How have technological developments affected our knowledge about the senses?

© Putting it into Practice. Artwork and Design © Pearson Education Ltd, 2010

An inquiry into: Senses

The learning centres framework

The learning centres framework provides an effective way to structure inquiry, allowing students to work in groups, pairs or individually to investigate different aspects of the unit. Depending on the space and time available, the learning centres shown here can be organised to address different lines of inquiry simultaneously, or to focus on one aspect at a time with activities differentiated for a range of abilities.

Senses centre
What are our senses?

Function centre
How do our sense work?

Geography centre
How can we use our senses to find out about different places?

Language centre
How can we describe what we see, hear, touch, smell, taste?

Mathematics centre
How do our senses help us with mathematics?

Art centre
How can we use our senses in art?

Sight centre
What can we see?

Hearing centre
What can we hear?

Touch centre
What can we feel?

Smell centre
What can we smell?

Taste centre
What can we taste?

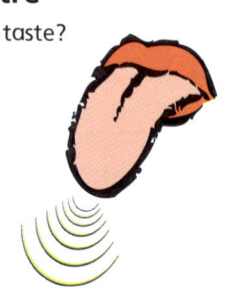

Nerve centre
How do our senses work together?

© Putting it into Practice. Artwork and Design © Pearson Education Ltd, 2010

An inquiry into: Senses

The unit of inquiry planner

The unit of inquiry planner provides an outline for teaching the unit of inquiry, identifying concepts, skills, knowledge and attitudes to be addressed, as well as key questions, activities, assessments and resources. For PYP schools, it focuses on the organising theme(s) indicated.

Central idea
Our senses are the main way we find out about the world.

Teacher: _____

Title: An inquiry into: Senses
Date: 6–8 weeks

Organising theme(s) to receive major emphasis

What do we want to learn?

Key Questions
1) What are our senses?
2) How can we use them?
3) How can we take care of them?

Concepts
we want students to understand:
- perception
- investigation
- sight
- hearing
- touch
- taste
- smell

Skills
we want students to be able to:
- ask questions
- observe
- listen

Knowledge
we want students to know about:
- the five senses
- sensory compensation
- sensory illusions
- camouflage

Attitudes
we want students to develop a sense of:
- curiosity
- safety
- responsibility
- empathy

How best will we learn?

Learning experiences

Tuning in activities
- I Robot
- Sense by sense
- Senses walk
- Safety aspects
- How the senses work (i and ii)

Investigating and exploring activities
- Student-initiated inquiries
- Senses Centres:
  - Sight centre – key questions, vocabulary, equipment and activities
  - *Camouflage* – hide the shapes
  - *Illusions (i and ii)* – tricking our senses
  - Hearing centre – key questions, vocabulary, equipment and activities
  - Sound waves – a role-play activity
  - Measuring sound – learning about frequency and amplitude
  - Smell and taste centres – key questions, vocabulary, equipment and activities
  - Ordering investigations – plan an investigation of different properties
  - Touch centre – key questions, vocabulary, equipment and activities
  - *Touch test* – test different materials with different body parts
  - *Quality webs (i, ii and iii)* – use these to evaluate different properties of sight, hearing, taste, smell and touch

Student questions

Action project

How can we show what we've learned?

Assessment opportunities

Senses Walk – an open-ended pre- and post-unit assessment
Class record sheet to show learning gains for each student
Using our senses – a formative assessment used to assess and record learning from individual activities throughout the unit. It also includes an individual student reflection.

Self assessment

Using our senses – a formative assessment used to assess and record learning from individual activities throughout the unit. It also includes an individual student reflection.

Outcomes

© Putting it into Practice. Artwork and Design © Pearson Education Ltd, 2010

An inquiry into: Senses

Resources

For a complete list of books, websites and activities, please visit: www.puttingitintopractice.com

Reflection

Teachers

Students

Weekly planner

An inquiry into: Senses

Teacher: _____   Title: _____
Organising theme(s) to receive major emphasis   Date: _____

Unit of Inquiry

Central idea

What do we want to learn?

Key Questions

Concepts
We want students to understand:

Skills
We want students to be able to:

Knowledge
We want students to learn about:

Attitudes
We want students to develop a sense of:

Student questions

How best will we learn?

Learning experiences

Action project

How can we show what we've learned?

Assessment opportunities

Self assessment

Outcomes

© Putting it into Practice. Artwork and Design © Pearson Education Ltd, 2010

An inquiry into: Senses

Resources

Reflection

Students

Teachers

Weekly planner

An inquiry into: Senses

Putting it into practice with parents

General guidelines

Working with parents is a fundamental part of teaching and if you can encourage the right level of involvement, they can be a valuable resource. These ideas are to help you to help them help their children! Parents should not be expected to teach new concepts or skills to their children – their support will be most successful if it helps students:

- prepare for new learning at school; for example, learning key vocabulary, gathering relevant pictures, interviewing family members
- practice skills; for example, recording information, generating questions, giving a class presentation
- extend the breadth and depth of their learning; for example, following personal lines of inquiry, investigating certain aspects in more detail, exploring new connections.

Briefly explain the nature of inquiry to them: parents may not have learned this way themselves, so they may not understand its value as a methodology and it may seem to be in conflict with the culture and education system of their home country.

Some key points you might want to include:

- inquiry is one learning method used alongside many others
- inquiry is supported by extensive educational and neurological research
- inquiry is a set of skills that become better as students practice
- inquiry can help students to process large amounts of complex information
- inquiry can help students be more independent learners
- inquiry can help students develop confidence and be better communicators.

Explain how valuable parental support can be in making connections between school and home, showing students the 'real life' relevance of their learning. Encouraging them to continue their learning at home can allow students to follow individual lines of inquiry to an extent that may not be feasible in mixed groups at school and is excellent preparation for lifelong learning. However simple or complex the task, try to give clear and specific written instructions about what to do, the due date, the product you expect and the amount of help parents should give.

Ideas for An inquiry into: Senses

- play I-Spy – either "with my little eye something beginning with…" or "something big and green…"
- encourage observation on a large and small scale, close and distant
- have a 'red' day when you look for everything that is red
- play I-Hear – either "with my little ear something beginning with…" or "something close and loud…"
- listen to stories, music and rhymes, both familiar and new
- try to identify different instruments and voices when listening
- play blindfold touch games, e.g. trying to guess letters or numbers 'drawn' on the palm of the hand or on the back, or made from sandpaper
- sort the cutlery drawer or pairs of socks by touch only
- name and describe different textures, e.g. soft, fluffy blanket; cold, smooth car door
- teach a range of adjectives to describe smells, e.g. strong, pungent, sweet, aromatic, perfumed, fragrant, smoky, fishy, etc
- play the 'Where am I?' smell game – 'I can smell…' Where am I?
- play the 'Smell Detector' game – be the first to detect and identify smells as you walk down the street, round shopping centres, at school, etc
- teach a range of adjectives to describe tastes, e.g. sweet, sour, bitter, salty, spicy, etc
- compare the taste and texture of raw and cooked foods (e.g. carrot, apple, bread); hot and cold foods (e.g. milk, egg, cheese)
- encourage tasting during cooking, e.g. "Does this sauce need more tomato paste?"
- teach the care, health and safety of the senses

An inquiry into: Senses

Senses centre

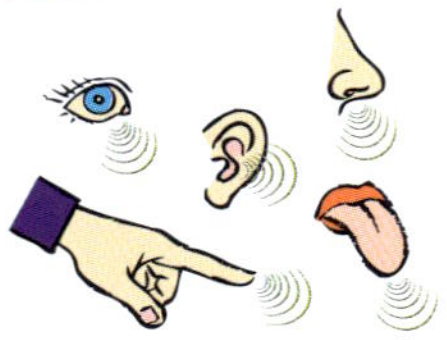

Key question
- What are our senses?

Further questions
- What is sight?
- What is hearing?
- What is touch?
- What is smell?
- What is taste?
- What is the 'sixth sense'?

Key vocabulary
sight
hearing
touch
smell
taste
nerves
eye
ear
skin
fingers
nose
mouth
tongue

Equipment
- books and posters about the senses

Recording ideas
- write down or draw 10 things you can see
- draw what you are wearing and label each thing with adjectives that describe how they look and feel
- record and chart survey results

Exploration activities
- look around the classroom and name all the things you can see in one minute
- close your eyes and listen then draw two things you can hear, one inside the classroom and one outside
- describe how the things you are wearing feel, e.g. soft, smooth, rough, tight, shiny
- think of a smell you like and another smell you don't like – compare with your friend
- draw your favourite food then ask 10 people if they also like that taste
- for each sense, draw some things you use them for each day
- do a survey to find out which sense people think is most important
- design a symbol for each sense

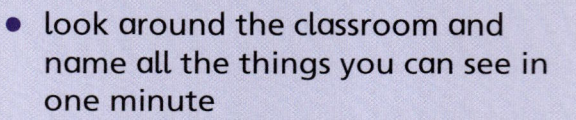

An inquiry into: Senses

Colourful shades

Choose a colour and try to find different shades. Use them to create a picture in the box.

My colour is: ☐

I used ☐ different shades.

Senses: Early Years Summarising activity 1

An inquiry into: Senses

Making sense of our senses

> Choose the right sense to match the words.

| hear | taste | | see |
| smell | | touch | |

eye eyelid sight	ear eardrum sound	fingers skin nerves	nose nostril breathe	tongue mouth tatsebuds

Senses: Lower Primary Inquiry activity 1

An inquiry into: Senses

Sense diagram

Choose **one** of the senses from in the list. Tick the one you choose and draw a labelled diagram to show how it works.

- sight
- hearing
- touch
- smell
- taste

Senses: Lower Primary Summarising activity 1
© Putting it into Practice. Artwork and Design © Pearson Education Ltd, 2010

An inquiry into: Senses

How our senses work

Read the information about each sense. Choose one sense and draw a simple diagram to show how it works.

Sight
The eye is like a camera: it works only when light comes into it. Both the camera and the eye have a lens to focus. Just as the camera keeps the pictures on film, disc or in the eye, the pictures are "retained" by the retina, and then passed to the brain as nerve signals.

Hearing
The ear works by detecting tiny vibrations in the air. The vibrations are amplified by the ear's internal structure, which includes the drum and the cochlea. The cochlea has tiny hairs that respond to the vibrations and turn them into nerve signals that go to the brain.

Smell
The nasal passages are lined with chemical detectors, which are activated by different sets of chemicals that travel through the air. It only takes a tiny amount of the chemical (measured in parts per million) to trigger the detectors. When they do trigger, they send nerve signals to the brain.

Taste
The tongue has chemical detectors (like those in the nose) near its surface. As with the nose these activated chemical detectors turn the reaction into nerve signals to the brain. The main difference between taste and smell is that a different nerve is used to send the data to the brain.

Touch
The body has a wiring system (nerves). At the end of the nerves are receptors – different kinds of receptors that respond to different kinds of stimuli. Our bodies are covered in these touch-sensitive receptors. In some parts of the body, such as the finger tips, which have a high concentration of receptors. This is good for high definition detection of surfaces and textures. When a receptor is activated it turns the mechanical contact into nerve signals that are sent to the brain.

Senses: Upper Primary Inquiry activity 1

An inquiry into: Senses

Taste tests

Choose four different foods to test.
Write them here and colour each box to make a key.

1. _____
2. _____
3. _____
4. _____

Choose five different taste qualities and write them on the quality web below.
Now taste each food and put a coloured dot on each of the branches to show the strength of the quality in that food.
Finally, use a ruler to join the dots with the appropriate colour for each food.

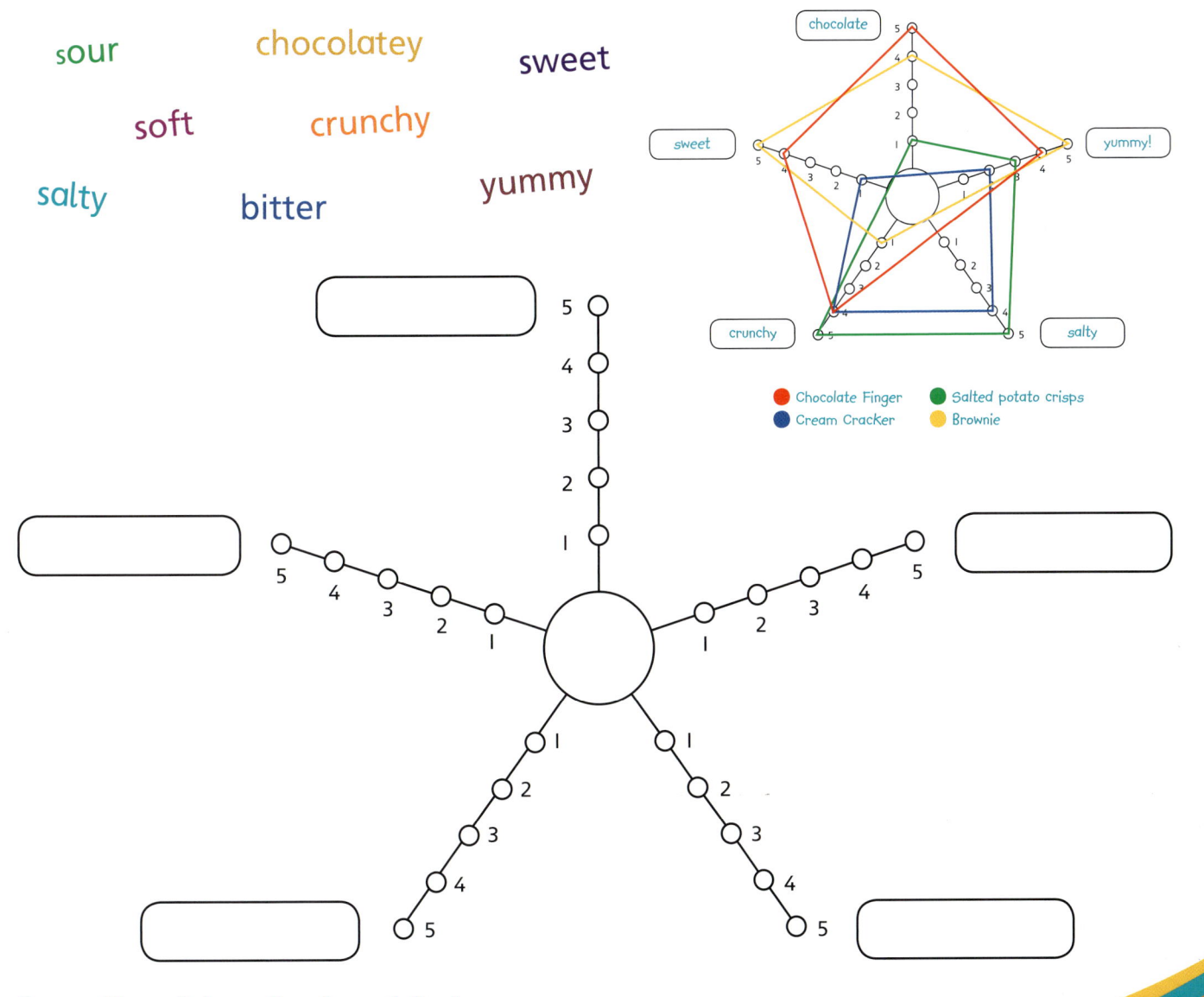

sour   chocolatey   sweet
soft   crunchy
salty   bitter   yummy

Example web (with labels: chocolate, sweet, crunchy, salty, yummy!):
- Chocolate Finger
- Cream Cracker
- Salted potato crisps
- Brownie

Senses: Upper Primary Inquiry activity 6

© Putting it into Practice. Artwork and Design © Pearson Education Ltd, 2010